Dream Oil Rig Job

The only guide that you will ever need to get your dream job on oil rig the easy way

AMARPREET SINGH

THE THOUGHT FLAME
TURNING SPARK INTO FLAME

info@thethoughtflame.com

www.thethoughtflame.com

Table of Contents

Introduction 1

Chapter One: Different Types of Jobs on Oil Rigs and What You Need To Land One 3

Chapter Two: Some Good Skills to Have and Where to Find Jobs on an Oil Rig..................14

Chapter Three: Life on an Oil Rig and What Every Newbie Needs To Know...................... 27

Chapter Four: The Truth About The Oil Rig Job Salary.................................... 33

Conclusion 37

About Us 39

Author 41

<u>Introduction</u>

If you are looking for a career that is fast growing and is one that is very high in demand, it really doesn't get any better than within the oil and gas industry. Today there are hundreds of both men and women that work on various oil rigs only 6 months out of the year and they still manage to make more money than most top earning professionals today. What is more is that these men and women are all able to do this with little to no experience necessary. Most of them never even go on to college either.

In order to work on an oil rig, regardless if it is land based or floating in the ocean, all you need is three things: a hard working mentality, driving dedication and a strong desire to make as much money as you want. If you have these three things, you can land a high paying and growing career in no time.

This eBook is one of the most comprehensive guide that you will find on how to find the perfect oil rig job for you. As long as you follow everything in this book to a T, I am 100% confident that you will be able to work on an oil rig in no time.

So, what are you waiting for? Let's get you started so you can get on an oil rig in no time!

Chapter One: Different Types of Jobs on Oil Rigs and What You Need To Land One

Just like with any industry that is available today and that does not require you to have previous experience, you will need to climb the ladder in order to make the big bucks in the industry. That's right, you will have to first start at the bottom of the food chain in order to become the big man or woman on campus in the future. Do not worry. Every person who tries to get into this industry have to do it and this is something most people are not aware of when going into it.

So, what drove you to considering getting a job on an oil rig? Was it the fact that you heard you could make a on of money in the industry just by working for a few short months? If so, I wouldn't be surprised. Before learning about the actual industry myself I too heard stories of workers earning up to $300,000 a year in just a few short months.

The truth of the matter is, that while yes you can earn a ton of money in just a short amount of time on an oil rig, you will first need to make the minimum amount that you can in an entry level position before you can truly make the big bucks and you will need to work harder than most people have to in regular jobs.

While working on oil rig is certainly one of the most exciting and interesting kinds of jobs that you can find out there today, there is a lot of demand that this job calls for. Not only do you have to be physically fit, but your mind needs to be fit as well to handle the stress this job will put on you. The truth is this job, as exciting as it can be, it really is not meant for everyone. Only certain people will thrive in this job and before you score a job on a rig, you need to ask yourself if you actually have what it takes to do this job and to do it right the first time.

So, what kind of jobs can you get on an oil rig and what do you have to do to land one of these dream jobs? You will learn exactly that in this chapter and what you can do to get the job that you want.

Type of Jobs On An Oil Rig

1. Floorhand

Although not considered to be one of the best jobs on an oil rig today, floodhands are still considered to be important members of the crew. While this position is considered to be the lowest member on the totem pole, they are responsible for completing jobs that are crucial to the successful operation of the rig. Floorhands generally report to their rig manager and are expected to help on the drilling floor during normal drilling operations.

Many people see this position as a bit disappointing and discouraging, but you must consider that if you are able to step onto an oil rig as a floorhand, you can work hard to get a much better position later by obtaining the proper certification, licenses, and training.

2. Roustabout

This position is also another entry level position in which many workers who do not have prior experience on an oil rig can apply for. Look at this position as an overpaid janitorial position with some hard labor involved. As a roustabout, workers are responsible for ensure that the entire rig is keep neat and tidy and that perform routine maintenance on the rig whenever necessary.

Some of the basic duties of a roustabout include but are not limited to:

1. Performing basic painting projects on the rig.

2. Monitoring equipment and machinery for routine maintenance.

3. Mixing the mud that is used during the drilling process.

4. Clean drilling tanks.

5. Much, much more.

On the rig roustabouts are expected to answer to their rig or drill manager, but this will ultimately depend on the company that they work for. This is a position that is perfect for those who have no experience and if you are person with little to no experience with working on an oil rig, this is the first position you will want to apply for.

3. Driller

Just as the name implies, a driller is mostly responsible for supervising and actually doing the drilling part of the whole operation, while making sure they are in perfect control of the machinery that they are using. As a driller you can expect to make decisions in real time related to the drilling process and will need to make sure that the entire process is done is a way that is both safe and efficient.

In order to qualify for this position on an oil rig, you will need to have either a few years of experience on a rig, have actual experience as a driller or have had enough years of study in the process of drilling in order to qualify. It is a tough job for many beginners to snag and it is not one that beginners should take lightly.

4. Cook

While I know this position may not be expected, it is one that is as equally important as the rest of the positions listed in this chapter. You may have heard the term, "An army doesn't march on an empty stomach." The same quote can be applied to those living and working on an oil rig.

This is one of the perfect positions for those looking to find a way through the door of an oil rig and is perfect for those who have absolutely no experience in the oil industry. Just as the title implies, the cook is responsible for cooking up all of the meals that the works will get throughout the time in the oil field. They are also responsible for managing all of the kitchen staff that is on the rig. While it may not seem like much, this is one of the most important jobs on the rig itself and it is one that many people tend to take for granted.

5. Derrickhand

Equally as important as the driller, the derrickhand is responsible for ensuring that the driller is raising and lowering the drill pipe, casing of the drill and collars, and maintaining the perfect amount of mud around the drill in a safe and efficient manner. Think of the derrickhand as the second in command on the drilling floor and is the person that is in full command if the driller is not available on the floor.

There are a few requirements for this position to ensure a good fit for it such as comfortable working from great heights for a long period of time and must be physically fit as ensure the drill is properly working and doing what it is supposed to do is very labor intensive.

6. The Rig Manager

The rig manager is in charge of, you guessed it, managing the rig and all that entails with making sure it runs smoothly on a daily basis. It is the rig managers job to ensure that all safety protocols are being followed on the rig while make sure that all of the operations are being completed in a timely manner.

Some of the responsibilities of a rig manager include creating weekly work schedules, maintaining the rig to the best of their ability, making sure the rig is being repaired when it needs to be, constantly monitoring the expenses and costs that are used to operate the rig while drilling and making sure to hire the appropriate subcontractors that they need for the project.

7. The Tool Pusher

The tool pusher is a crewmember that has the highest ranking on the drilling floor on any rig, whether it is floating on the water or in the middle of dry land. The tool pusher is responsible for many things such as supervising the drilling equipment that is used to supervising the crew to ensure all the work that needs to be done with the drill gets done properly.

In order to qualify for this position, you will need to have a few years of experience under your belt with working with an oil drill before. The more experience you have the better. However, you can still work towards this position within the oil industry, even if you start from the very bottom.

If you are just getting into the world of drilling, you cannot expect to be hired as a rig manager right off the back. You need to have the appropriate experience ranging from 5 years and above while working on other oil rigs and must have the right managerial experience under your belt as well.

There are many different types of jobs that you can apply for when trying to land a dream job on an oil rig and a few of them do not require you to have any experience beforehand. While it is harder to land higher ranking jobs such as the Rig manager or the Derrickhand, but even if you start from the very bottom, it is possible to work towards these positions and to be promoted fast in little to no time at all.

Chapter Two: Some Good Skills to Have and Where to Find Jobs on an Oil Rig

Now that you know about the different positions that you can apply for when looking for a job on an oil rig, there are a few things that you will need to do first in order to ensure that you get the job that you want. There are a few skills that you will want to have to help make you stand out above the rest of the applicants and that will have a rig manager begging for you to join the team.

In this chapter you will learn exactly what skills you should have under your belt to help you get the dream oil rig job that you want and where exactly all of the oil rigs jobs are so you know where to start looking for them.

What Are Good Skills To Have Under Your Belt?

While it is not necessary for you to have any experience when apply to work on an oil rig, there are some things that you will have to learn and do before even thinking about applying for a job. As you may or may not be aware of, there is a certain amount of risks that does into working on one of these rigs. You have probably heard about a few horror stories of accidents gone wrong on one of these rigs and the truth of the matter is that there is real truth to these stories. Working on a rig is extremely dangerous work, but hey, that is why people make the big bucks on them.

So, once you understand the real risks that goes with working on one of these rigs, what can you do to show hiring managers that you have what it takes to work on one?

1. Get a Health Physical

There is a lot of physical labor that you will have to do when working on an oil rig and this is what prevents a hiring manager on a rig from hiring someone who cannot live up to the task of working on a rig. Getting a health physical will a hiring manager that you are not only as healthy as a horse, but that you are capable to dealing with the strain of lifting heavy machinery and working 12 to 14 hours on end for as long as you are on the oil rig. Before even applying for a job, make sure that you get this done first.

2. Have Some Additional Training

Let's face it, having extra training in the oil industry will not hurt you, it will only help you. There are many training course that you can take and that will help to prepare you for life on an oil rig. You can take training classes in handling hazardous materials, health and safety on a rig, first aid, working at extreme heights, lifting equipment training and helicopter safety. There are endless training course available out there and these courses will help you to stand out above any other applicants.

3. Apprenticeships

What better way is there to begin working on a rig then actually getting some actual experience on one? One of those most common ways people land jobs on these huge rigs is by becoming an apprentice to someone who works on one. Most oil rig employers prefer those who have apprenticeships anyway because it shows that they have prior experience and know what they have to do while working on an oil rig.

As an apprentice there are many duties that you can expect to perform such as starting out in an entry level position and learning more about the rig itself. You may start off as a roustabout for a while before moving up through the ranks. As an apprentice you will learn many things from welding, to lowering a pipe, maintaining a drill pipe and even learning some important safety protocols that you will need to know anyway.

The best way to find an apprenticeship is to go online. There are many forums and websites out there designed to help you find the perfect apprenticeship that will fit your needs and get you working on an oil rig in no time.

While you can certainly get your foot in the door by landing a good, high-paying entry-level oil rig position with no experience, you should understand that getting a diploma or certificate in a pertinent technical trade (e.g. plumber, electrician or mechanic) will help jumpstart your exciting and new career in the oil industry at an entirely different level, and position yourself to earn a lot more money initially.

The Common Requirements to Working on an Oil Rig

While it is incredibly easy to land a job on an oil rig, there are a few requirements that most hiring managers will have in place to make sure only the right candidates are selected for the job. Here are a few requirements that most oil rigs commonly ask for.

1. Degree Level-most hiring managers on oil rigs require that you have at least a high school diploma even for the most basic jobs. While it is required for many oil rig jobs, there are a fair few that do not require it at all. It will all depend on the company and hiring manager.

2. Experience-most hiring managers will ask that you have at least some basic knowledge of how a rig operates on a daily basis and how most of the equipment used on a rig is used. Of course this may not be necessary for some rigs, but the more you know about what it takes to run an oil rig, the better your chances are to getting the job that you want.

3. A Few Technical Skills-a few hiring managers may ask that you have a few technical skills under your belt. Some technical skills that most hiring managers look for today may include how to operate heavy machinery, some basic mechanic skills such as welding and some knowledge of how to operate any computers that may be on the rig.

There are different ways that you can gain the necessary technical skills that most managers look for in the form of training courses or apprenticeships. You options are virtually limitless.

4. Some Extra Requirements-there are a few extra things that many hiring managers on oil rigs look for today such as the ability to pass a drug screening (you are going to be working around some heavy duty machinery so this should no surprise for anybody), make sure that you pass any prior medical screenings, a clean criminal history background and the ability to work more than your average 8 hours a day.

As long as you have all of these prior requirements, you should not have a problem getting the dream oil rig job that you want.

Where to Find Oil Rig Jobs

Now that you know what kind of oil rig jobs you can land, what you need to get one and what special training you should undergo beforehand, it is time to actually help you find a job on an oil rig.

Now, the thing that you have to understand here is that an in order to find a job on an oil rig, you need to go to where the jobs are. There are a few places where companies are drilling for oil right at this moment such as within the United States itself, to off the shores of Alaska and even in the lone star state of Texas. However, your best chance to getting the dream job that you want is to look towards Texas.

It is no secret that Texas has long been known as one of the richest oil states in the USA and current statistics show that black gold in this region of the country is still not letting up. Here are some reasons why it is hailed as the richest places of oil in the US today:

1. Last year alone, the average number of approved drilling permits in the state was about 1,600 permits being created per month. Within a twelve-month period alone, that translates to about 19,200 possibly existing oil wells that can be found just within the state of Texas! How does this apply to you? To put it simply-there are more jobs for people here

than anywhere else, especially if they are looking to start a career in the oil industry.

2. As of 2011, Texas alone has been able to produce over 4 million barrels of oil. This is a staggering increase and will ensure that the national pile of oil will help to sustain the country in the future, even if oil is not found within any offshore deposits.

3. The harvesting of natural gas is holding steady, with an average of 530 million barrels being mined per month. Although there has been no increase in the recent months it does not mean that the production of oil is slowing down in the slightest. Consistent production of oil means that people will still be hired on oil rigs in the coming years and the increase of new positions every month is almost 100% guaranteed.

Now can you see why I recommend Texas as one of the best places to land a job on an oil rig today? With the booming industry and an endless amount of oil rig jobs, it should be relatively easy for you to land the job that you want.

What Oil Companies Are Hiring Right Now?

Currently, there are over 5,000 companies around the world drilling for oil, most of which are working in installations located in oil rich parts of the world. These oil rig jobs are prevalent in different countries such as the United States, Canada, Saudi Arabia, Kuwait, Iraq, the United Arab Emirates, Venezuela and Nigeria.

Here's is a short list of ten of the most popular oil rig drilling companies in the world that are hiring right at this moment and this serves as a good reference point for those looking for information on the types of companies that provide a large supply of oil rig jobs:

1. Schlumberger

2. Halliburton

3. Saipem

4. Transocean

5. Baker

6. Hughes

7. Fluor

8. Weatherford International

9. BJ Services Company

10. Petrofac

11. China Oilfield Services Ltd.

It is important to note that most drilling companies that are located around different parts of the world today like to keep a low profile in public so it is not uncommon to have trouble finding job availabilities with this. Reach out to the company through traditional means if you are looking to apply for a position with them.

Chapter Three: Life on an Oil Rig and What Every Newbie Needs To Know

I know that once you begin reading about how much money you can make on an oil rig, you seem to not be able to think about anything else. I know for some that the reality of the kind of work that you will have to do or the living conditions that you may have to endure do not seem to heat any novice until they get to an oil rig.

This chapter is solely dedicated to helping you understand the kind of life you will be living once you begin working on an oil rig. Remember, this type of work is not meant for everybody and the more you understand about the position, the more you will know if you are cut out for this type of work.

The Truth of an Oil Rig Career

It is no secret that there is an ever-increasing demand for workers on oil rigs, whether they be land based or offshore. On an oil rig, the truth is that you can find a job practically anywhere. It is absolutely booming. However, living away from home for weeks on end, being isolated from the real world and working constantly in an environment that is stressful is something that can take a toll even on the most seasoned of workers.

The truth of the matter is that most people are drawn to this profession for its amazing benefits and attractive pay. However, you have to look at the bigger picture to know if this career is really the one that you are destined to be in.

1. Living Accommodations

Of course living accommodations will vary from oil rig to oil rig and each one will be different from the last. You will find different living quarters ranging from single rooms with basic bunk beds to impressive suite style rooms.

Living conditions have improved greatly from what they used to be many years ago and many of them can even meets surprising hotel standards. Remember, during your off time you will no doubt want to have a place that you will be able to call home and that you will be comfortable in to spend your relaxation time in.

Most rigs today have great accommodations and amenities where you can find that spending your free time is actually worthwhile. Many rigs are built to have satellite TV, free movies, wifi and even a gym. Of course like I said, some rigs will be different and may have little to no amenities other than the absolute basics.

2. Work Schedule

Now, this is one thing that many newbies, while they hear about it do not actually believe it until they begin their very first day of work on a rig. While there are many differences between companies, you can expect the work schedules to be very similar.

Most commonly schedules will have you work for about 14 days straight, with about 21 days that you have off or as long as 1 month off. You can expect to work approximately 80 to 100 hours per week and work one shift of 12 hours or more. Now while that may not seem like much, it will finally hit you during your first week.

Working 12 hours straights for 14 straight days is not easy, even for the simplest of jobs. However, working on a rig is different as most of the work is physically intense and you will strain muscles that you never know you had.

You will need to make sure that you can handle this type of work before you hurt yourself in the process.

3. The Reality of Being Isolated

If there is one aspect of working on a rig that doesn't fit most newbies, it is the fact that you are literally isolated from other people expect for the ones that you work with. This little fact can cause many crew members, even the experienced ones to lose it a bit as it is something that most people are not used to. Add in the fact that you could be working in claustrophobic conditions can add to the horrible feeling of isolation and make this is job that is simply not meant for most people.

The good part about being isolated from the public and only having the company of your co-workers is that you will become part of a special little family. When you work with others in conditions as dangerous as the ones that are on an oil rig and for so many hours, you will build a close relationship that even most families will never experience.

While living and working on an oil rig is a fairly dangerous career to have, the attractive pay and the relationship that you will build with your co-workers are aspects of this job that make it worthwhile. However, it is important to know these facts so as a greenhorn you will know exactly what you are getting yourself into.

Chapter Four: The Truth About The Oil Rig Job Salary

There is a lot of confusion when it comes to finding out exactly how much money your typical oil rig worker makes per year, regardless if they are on and offshore oil rig or a land based oil rig. There are so many misconceptions about the typical pay that there are many more rumors out there than the actual truth.

The first thing that you have to realize is that most oil rig employees have different jobs upon the rig and as such they may be paid differently than another employee. They all have different tasks and depending on how long they have been working for that particular company will play a role in how much money they make every year. The only real difference between every oil rig company out there and what determines how their employees are paid is what they are drilling for, whether is it natural gas, crude oil or black oil, also referred to as black gold.

Depending on how much experience a person has can add to the factors that determine a workers salary as well as their position within the oil rig. However, here are some helpful facts that may shed some light on this important aspect of this dangerous job.

Last year alone, the average salary for oil rig workers and other oil industry personnel was a whopping $ 99,175. Of course, that number is padded by the enormous paychecks for drilling consultants who pull in $ 235,586 a year or by the $ 139,868 reservoir engineers make each year.

However, even without taking the highly skilled workers into account, the average oil rig worker with under a year of experience pulls in a cool $

66,923. Even the lowest position workers on a rig—the roustabout who performs general maintenance and physical labor requiring no experience— makes about $34,680, which is the median wage for practically all American workers. Other oil rig job types and their respective annual wages/ pay:

- Rotary drill operators make $ 58,540 per year
- A rig foreman makes $ 193,306 each year
- A mud engineer takes home $ 108,032 a year

As you can see, the pay is substantial throughout the entire oil industry; keeping in mind the amazing potential for advancement, it's easy to see why someone with no experience would certainly want to foray into this extremely lucrative industry where in just a few short years of receiving some intense on-the-job training, they could quite easily position themselves to command an impressive $ 100,000 a year or more salary throughout their exciting work career.

What you should take away from this is that while it is certainly possible to rake in the big bucks that a rig foreman or a deck manager makes, without the necessary experience, I wouldn't be begging for that much money anytime soon. If you are able to apply for a great managerial position within the company itself, the reality is that you will most likely be granted a position that will require you to do a lot of heavy lifting. That being said the best way to earn the highest salary that you can on an oil rig is to gain as many skills as humanely possible and by making sure you have the necessary strength and endurance to live up to the task.

Conclusion

Oil rig jobs are not only very demanding in the physical sense, but they also require you to work an endless amount of hours straight through and to work in conditions that are potentially life threatening. You will also need to be able to be comfortable with working in conditions where you will be exposed to great heights, so having no fear of heights or at risk to vertigo is an absolute must.

Remember, working on an oil rig requires you to be away from your family for long periods of time, as well as be exposed to a variety of different conditions. This job is not for the faint hearted or weak. Only the toughest and most healthy applicants will be able to score a job on one of these rigs and reap the rewards that come with working on one.

While it is not that difficult to get a job on an oil rig, there are a few things that you can do to improve your chances of being hired. Hopefully in this eBook you learned what some of those things were such as taking special training and where are the best places in the world to find oil rig job. I also hope that by reading this book that you understand whether or not you have what it takes to get a job on an oil rig. If you are serious about getting the dream oil rig job that you have always wanted, this guide can certainly help you achieve that.

About Us

The Thought Flame is committed to add value to its customers through various books, online courses and other resources. You can learn more about us and our books at www.thethoughtflame.com.

Don't forget to check out our amazing **online video courses** at www.thethoughtflame.com/courses/ to take your knowledge to another level.

To check out our **extraordinary collection of diet/cookbooks**, visit http://www.thethoughtflame.com/category/non-fictional/cookbooks/ .

As a part of our valued relationship with our customers, we keep providing you free promotional books, courses and other stuff on subscribing with us on our site. We have a strict anti-spam policy and assure you no spam mails will be sent to your mailbox.

To subscribe with us, visit

www.thethoughtflame.com.

Like our work and would like to say thanks?

Buy us a cup of coffee at

www.thethoughtflame.com/coffee/

Author

Amarpreet Singh is an avid learner and his passion for education has made him travel, work and study all across the world. He holds three masters degrees, including MBA, from top universities in Asia.

He is author of dozens of books, many of which are Amazon's bestseller, varying in various topics and categories. He also teaches many online courses having thousands of students across the world.

He has a keen interest in international affairs, economics, global poverty and politics, financial markets and entrepreneurship, and strives to be part of a community that shares the same passion.

He has worked as consultant with organizations like Airbus and The World Bank. He loves travelling and learning about new cultures, and has been fortunate to live/work/travel/study in countries like India, China, Korea, US, South Africa, Japan, Philippines, Singapore, Canada etc., and learn about the culture and lifestyle in each of them. To check out more of his work, visit www.thethoughtflame.com

www.ingramcontent.com/pod-product-compliance
Lightning Source LLC
Chambersburg PA
CBHW021445170526
45164CB00001B/405